A  Management & Client Satisfaction:

The Savvy Agent

Increase your Referrals and Eliminate Liability.

Courtesy of
The Lighthouse Group
Home Inspection Company
800-993-1791

P. Nathan Thornberry

Advanced Risk Management & Client Satisfaction: The Savvy Agent: Increase your Referrals and Eliminate Liability
P. Nathan Thornberry © 2015 P. Nathan Thornberry

ISBN 978-0-692-48601-6

Cover design Danii Bonebrake
Editing by Jenifer Costner

Project Manager: Nathan Ehman

Orders by U.S. trade bookstores and wholesalers. Please contact RWS: Tel: (800) 544-8156; Fax: (877) 307-7056. Printed in the United States of America. First Edition July 2015.

Table of Contents

This book is dedicated to all of the thousands of agents with whom we have worked in our careers who have given up their nights and weekends ensuring buyers & sellers are taken care of.

You play a much larger role in lives than you realize. I hope this book makes that role even more positive than ever before.

Sincerely,

P. Nathan Thornberry
www.Nathan.tv

Chapter 1
The Front Page of the Newspaper

When we talk about liability in any profession, the conversation is often one-dimensional and tends to focus solely on lawsuits.

You'll find this phenomenon exists in almost every industry, largely due to the attention frivolous lawsuits get in the media and some of the stories that get spread around without the full details. The reality is that lawsuits against agents are relatively rare and most are settled or dealt with before they ever really start.

So long as a real estate agent doesn't engage in fraud, deception, or venture into areas far outside their expertise, lawsuits are generally non-existent. The ones that do happen are either incredible exceptions, or fall into one of the following categories;

- *Misrepresentation regarding the condition of the property.*

- *Misrepresentation regarding flooding or leaks.*

- *Bodily Injury resulting from a property condition.*

- *Earnest/Escrow money disputes.*

These lawsuits are usually well under $25,000.00, many even end up in small claims court.

When it comes to big lawsuits, they are in almost every situation avoidable. Outright fraud, where a broker uses escrow funds or an agent sells a property that doesn't exist, Breach of Contract & Breach of Duty, where an agent simply gets in over their head or fails to follow basic ethics rules, and Consumer Protection Act violations are all things most agents do a pretty good job of avoiding. Sales managers do a great job of helping agents to avoid these issues as well and they usually spot the signs of shady deals quickly- another reason lawsuits are a rarity in real estate.

So if we pull out the crazy multi-million dollar lawsuits against slick developer salespeople selling condos that will never be built and the unfortunate circumstances where a broker uses an escrow account as his own personal piggy bank, we are left with a very infrequent group of small-scale issues where buyers feel they have been led astray...and almost every time it has to do with the condition of the home they just bought.

This is where the "gaps" of real estate come into play- gaps that create unnecessary liability and harm your referral base.

Gaps exist everywhere there is a juncture between participants and components in the real estate transaction and the home ownership process- and this includes everyone.

When it comes to direct participants in a transaction, there isn't a gap that can't be eradicated.

Before we get into identifying the gaps and how to eliminate them completely, let's talk a little about why we do this. As already stated, legal liability is almost a non-issue in real estate, so why should we be concerned about these things at all?

The first reason is simple: We don't want to become the exception to the rule. It doesn't take much to push someone over the edge, and being involved in over 100,000 real estate transactions monthly I can tell you from experience that for some it does not take hardly anything at all.

The second reason is the real reason: Success. More specifically, keeping negative client experiences from preventing success.

I come from a real estate family and my grandfather, Don Thornberry, was a Re/Max agent until the day he died. He sold tens of millions in real estate annually. He had a great reputation throughout the Indy Metro area, and I think it had a lot to do with one thing he would always tell me:

"Don't do anything you wouldn't want on the front cover of the newspaper."

It sounds cliché, it sounds old school, and it is, but it is a great rule to live by. The only thing left undefined and seems to be changing by the day is what exactly one wouldn't want on the front cover of the paper in today's media driven world.

I believe just about any publicity is good publicity with one glaring exception: Negative Testimonials.

Let's put ourselves in the client's shoes for a moment and we will assume that you helped them find a house, write an offer, get through all contingencies, and each step of the way they did everything you suggested to a T.

Now let's say it is a week after they move in and something happens where home ownership has become a financial nightmare in the thousands of dollars, unexpectedly. Let's assume as well that this occurrence is a normal cost of home ownership and just an unfortunate circumstance.

Assuming there is no foul play, it is unlikely the new home owners will hire an attorney to come after you...they just spent a lot of time with you and likely had some level of trust before engaging your services. You may even know them on a personal level. They may call you or write you a letter, and when they do there are really only four potential outcomes in most scenarios;

1. You write them a check.

2. You make phone calls and fight for your clients with vendors and parties to the transaction that may or may not actually have responsibility to the issue.

3. You explain to the client that this is an unfortunate circumstance and you're sorry about their problems.

4. You already have a solution.

Most agents will stop short of writing a check, especially if the amount is in the thousands, so outcome number one is almost irrelevant.

Outcome number two may or may not yield great results for the client, but it actually does more harm than good in most cases to beat your partners over their heads.

A simple explanation to the client, outcome number three, is the default position in most cases and the result more often than any of the other scenarios. It's a natural tendency as salespeople to think we can talk our way through a problem and have everyone thinking as positive as we are (which couldn't be further from the truth).

Outcome number four is what the thoughtful experts have at the ready 99.9% of the time, and this is why they are incredibly successful.

In this book we will identify the gaps, identify the solutions, and show you how to implement them effortlessly- at no cost to anyone in almost every case. These are the simplest ways to have a solution at the ready and candidly every solution described in this book should be something you are aware of as a real estate professional.

Chapter 2
Identifying Gaps

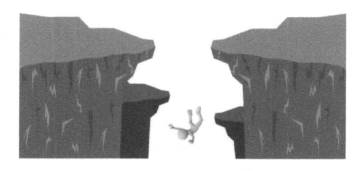

Throughout my career as a service provider to the real estate industry, I've had the pleasure of working with literally thousands of agents. Some I know personally better than others, many know our salespeople (rightfully) much better than I.

Some go way back. Family friend and a local real estate legend would be in that category, and if I had to pick one agent who was not only excellent at identifying gaps but also solving them and truly leveraging this ability into generating more referrals, he would be world champion. I'm sure there are others who do this job very well for their clients, but his office is right here near our headquarters outside Indianapolis, so he is in the unique position of inviting me over for a "talk" every once in a while.

What he does at these "talks" is nothing short of brilliant. Here it is, step by step;

1. *Invite the vendor over to talk business. Schedule it out a few days. No one will ever turn you down (mortgage, title, inspection, warranty...without exception).*

2. *Ask the vendor what is new. This step serves two purposes. First, you get caught up on what's offered. Second, the vendor gets in the mood to deal- which always benefits your clients.*

3. *Let the vendor know they're not the only player in the market. Even if you like them, even if you're friends, even if your families have been in the industry together for 30 years or longer (as is the case with this agent and myself)...let them know you are*

there for the best deal for your clients and solving pain points for them.

4. *Go over any issues you've had with that vendor or others for the last year, even minor issues, and discuss how to improve on them.*

5. *Give the vendor a task to do, and hold them accountable on the deliverables. Maybe it is custom order forms, a new package...whatever it may be. Of course the more transactions you do the better, and the more customizable this offering should be.*

That's pretty much it. Surprisingly, few agents ever take this opportunity to sit down with a vendor and figure out how to increase their customer satisfaction and consequential referrals, despite the free meal that would likely come with it.

If you've only sold a few houses, you may not know the pain points yet- so let's get straight to it.

There are basically four vendors you deal with in the course of a transaction on a high level- mortgage, title, home inspection, and warranty. When it comes to title/escrow services, things are pretty cut and dry. Either they return phone calls and emails promptly, or they don't. Either they have the right location for your business and are available for your needs, or not. Either they know their math and how to prepare the closing docs or they don't.

If they deliver great service and perhaps great cookies as well, you're probably pretty happy with your title company.

Mortgage brokers are about the same. Either they offer great rates and minimal closing costs, or they don't. Either they get the deal done, or they don't. When they don't get the deal done, we move on to the next guy. Pretty simple.

With experience in this industry, you'll find the right title and mortgage people to suggest to your clients.

Home Inspection on the other hand, is a great deal more complex, and the stakes are a lot higher.

Consider this: When was the last time a client called you to tell you that they were dissatisfied with their mortgage lender and wanted you to take action and get their payment dropped by hundreds of dollars?

It sounds ridiculous and it is. Perhaps it has happened a few times, but generally when a new homeowner gets their first mortgage statement there are not a lot of surprises. They expected a $4,000.00 mortgage payment and this is exactly what they have to look forward to.

The math, like the expectations, are finite. You do your best to maintain great relationships with Title and Mortgage providers, and hold them accountable to basic service levels.

In home inspection, things are totally different. Expectations are incredibly varied and the pitfalls range in the thousands. Same goes for home warranties.

Let me give you one example of a gap that involves both the home inspection and the home warranty, one that could cost your client thousands and cost you countless referrals.

This is an example of a real estate "gap".

Buyer gets a home inspection from company A. In the course of the home inspection, nothing out of the ordinary is uncovered. Home was built in the early 90's, on a slab, first time home buyer. Seller agrees to a few minor repair needs and buyer closes on the home with 10% down which represents the majority of their savings.

Shortly after moving into the home, buyer experiences a backed up sewer line affecting the entire home. They make a home warranty claim, only to find that coverage stops at the perimeter of the home and clogs are not covered. A call to the home inspector reveals that no testing of the sewer line occurred outside of running water on the day of the inspection.

Buyer calls you to report their difficult situation. The plumber has confirmed the line has a significant root intrusion and it needs to be replaced, at a cost of thousands of dollars.

What can you do about this?!?

This gap in real estate, a huge disappointment to buyers, happens thousands of times every year all over North America. It is the source of several hundred small claims cases against agents and home inspectors as well.

The worst part for you as an agent is that you really feel terrible for your client when this happens. If having sewage back up into their dream home wasn't enough, now they have to spend thousands of dollars dealing with the consequences.

In Chapter 1, we identified the four potential outcomes of any "real estate gap" and corresponding complaint. Let's put all four in context of this sewer line issue;

1. You write them a check.

2. You make phone calls and fight for your clients with vendors and parties to the transaction that may or may not actually have responsibility to the issue.

3. You explain to the client that this is an unfortunate circumstance and you're sorry about their problem.

4. You already have a solution.

Outcome #1 stings, and most agents don't immediately pull their checkbook out and write a check for thousands of dollars. I realize you may have the ability, but this is hardly the way to run a business from a fiscal perspective.

Outcome #2 is futile. In 16 years and over a quarter million claims I've handled across the country I've never heard of a single occasion where an agent was able to convince a home inspector or warranty company [that excludes sewer lines which is most all of them] to cover the issue. Maybe it has happened, but I would not count on it.

Outcome #3 is what happens around 80% of the time in the market today. With any luck, that number will decrease, but for now most agents are armed with only excuses and sympathy for their client. They certainly don't enjoy this position but it is all they feel that they have.

Outcome #4 is what happens around 20% of the time, and it results in happier clients and more referrals.

In your market for example, clients that utilize certain home inspectors are protected from this gap

with a policy known as SewerGard. Here's the logo
to look for:

It may sound too good to be true, but when you use
an inspector that has prepared the solution ahead
of time, your transaction becomes a lot smoother.

Your client, simply by utilizing the inspector you did
your homework on, has a better outcome with less
gaps. If they move in and have a sewer line issue,
the repair is covered. This policy lasts for several
months after the inspection generally and can be
extended at a minimal cost.

Of course another solution would be to choose
Residential Warranty Services for your home
warranty- it is the only policy in real estate to cover
underground sewer, water, and gas lines. You can
find this policy at www.RWSwarranty.com.

Now put this scenario in the context of a marketing event. Say your client, living on the same street as a number of other homes with aging sewage lines, is having a backyard barbeque when mention is made of the work they just had done in their front yard.

How do you think that conversation should go?

I would prefer a very happy couple say "Our agent took great care of us and luckily we had coverage for the sewer line." It sure beats "This house is a money pit."

It is important to note that you should always look for the SewerGard logo. It's a policy backed by a licensed home warranty provider, not one backed by the home inspector himself. Home inspectors aren't regulated in any financial way and none carry insurance policies to cover these guarantees or have reserves to back up such a policy.

It is Chapter 2 and we have already saved your clients thousands of dollars on one of the most expensive and aggravating difficulties a homebuyer can have.

Gaps exist wherever unfortunate circumstances, complaints, and excuses reside in harmony. If you've been in this industry for long enough, you have experienced this phenomenon.

Grab a sheet of paper and write down three gaps you've experienced, particularly in the areas of home inspection and/or home warranty, and then continue on to the next chapter and beyond.

We will likely address all three you identified. We tested this theory on around a hundred real estate professionals like yourself before we published this book. If by chance we missed one, go to www.RealEstateMessageBoard.com and post your gap. You may just find a solution there and be made famous in our next book!

Chapter 3
The Mold Mess

The way we deal with mold, mold testing, and mold remediation in real estate is *insanity*...but it is getting better. In the mid to late 90's, there was a crisis in real estate, which caused another gap (actually, gaps plural). This gap was much wider than others and seemed to change by the day. Lawsuits were happening and they were big ones for around three to five years.

While this area of real estate is still changing, mold testing has finally, to the largest extent, stabilized. In the last chapter, we focused on a gap that occurred after closing- and this is where most of the gaps reside. Mold is unique in that it lives in both the pre-sale and post-closing arenas.

Twenty years ago, and unfortunately still the case with some mold testing providers today, we confused the marketplace. Home Inspectors, mold remediators, homeowner's insurance companies, and even real estate agents all played a role.

It started with a home buyer asking a question: *Do I need a mold test?*

This is where the agent came into play, and they didn't know how to answer. We basically handed the client a form to sign to reduce our liability and then told them to go to the internet, which was information overload.

Some sites said to test, some sites said not to, some said to treat mold yourself, others said to call in the professionals, some said mold was everywhere and minimized the problem, and others said you might die from it.

What a nightmare.

By the time the client actually got a mold test done, things took a turn for the worse. Home inspectors and mold testing professionals at the time were taking nothing but a report of spore counts from a lab and then "interpreting" the results and delivering it to the client with 2-3 pages of narratives that basically said nothing.

Now the remediators get involved. Armed with this long report, they then put together an extremely expensive proposal that involved turning the home into a scene from the movie *E.T.*

Homeowner's insurance providers put the final nail in the perception coffin by completely excluding mold from their policies (and being very loud about it), when they failed to understand the subject or why it was becoming an issue for them in courtrooms.

Here's the pre-sale gap mold presents to you and your client:

Should a client test or not, and what should that test look like?

You'll hear a lot of so-called experts say things like "you shouldn't test for mold because mold is a moisture issue. Address the moisture."

While there is a bit of truth in that statement, there's also a lot missing. First off, even if you deal with the moisture issue, you still want to clean up the mold. Second, identifying that it is in fact mold is the first step.

The other thing missing here is the context of the real estate transaction. Our reality, as real estate professionals, is that the home is about to change hands and we have an inspection contingency to deal with. Rather than make a blanket statement as to whether or not testing is a good idea, we can just identify the legitimate reasons for which a test should be done. That way we can talk about mold in a very straight-forward way without making blanket statements that can easily be refuted.

Here are the Reasons to Test for Mold

#1 Mold or suspected mold is visible on a surface. At this point surface testing is a good idea, as it will aid in the inspection response and ensuring the seller handles the mold issue appropriately. As a follow-up to mold remediation work, Indoor Air Quality testing may be a great option to ensure work was completed to your client's satisfaction.

#2 Work was done recently or it smells. If there was mold remediation work done recently or the house has that "musty odor" we have all come to know all too well, a simple Indoor Air Quality test will give the buyer peace of mind or uncover an issue that may not be evident in the course of a visual inspection. Either way, the return on investment is good.

#3 Allergies and health issues. Some clients have issues (or kids with issues) and they know it. Maybe they see a physician or allergist for these issues. Either way, no reason for them to chance it. An Indoor Air Quality test is cheap, fast, and cost effective.

I'm not a proponent of blanket testing every home for mold, the return on investment would be negative and it simply isn't necessary. If you keep these three reasons for mold testing listed above in mind, it will help you better advise your client.

Now comes the important part- *What should the test look like?*

The mold test results should state very clearly whether normal levels of mold were detected or elevated levels were detected. In the case of a surface sample, they should simply state whether growth or no growth was present.

Neither you, your client, nor your inspector should ever have to take into consideration the spore counts or what type of molds are present. You shouldn't have to learn about "Beltrania" or "Curvularia" or "Myxomycetes". These counts should be included in the report, but they should be secondary to the interpreted results.

In parts of North America where Radon testing is common, think of mold testing in the same way. We are either within acceptable levels or we are not. There is either growth or there isn't.

Depending on those results, action should be taken or no action is necessary.

Here's the tricky part for you as a real estate agent and for your client: Picking a mold testing professional has as much to do with the laboratory they utilize as anything. Out of the hundreds of labs out there, only a very small handful offer the results based testing I've described above.

Many of the leading home inspectors and mold testing companies utilize one of them- InspectorLab out of Fort Lauderdale, which services real estate transactions throughout North America. Results are quick, clear, and accurate. Look for this logo:

This will simplify your life in the course of the transaction. Figuring out what the results mean and having endless phone calls and just as much internet research by the client, making a "mold mess" out of your transaction, is a thing of the past.

To recap:

1. Only recommend testing for mold when it's visible, there is cause for concern, or the future occupants have health issues to be concerned with.

2. There's no reason to test every single house.

3. Mold testing should be simple, with results that clearly state whether there is a problem to address or not.

If we handle the mold issue on this level, the transaction will go much smoother. Don't try to avoid the issue, let's deal with it head on- your clients will thank you for it.

After the test, there's either an issue to address in the inspection response or not. If there is, talk to your inspector about post-remediation testing.

Now let's talk about the post-closing gap in Mold:

Accountability.

Part of the problem with mold in the real estate transaction is how everyone runs away from it. The insurance company excludes it, the basic home inspection excludes it, real estate brokers have the client sign a disclosure form... no wonder the client is concerned.

The last straw (and another source of confusion) is when the client gets results and they have a big disclosure on them that basically says mold can grow tomorrow and the results of this test and the paper they're written on are worthless immediately after they are issued.

So here's another gap. Client moves in, after doing everything they should have and then some. They had a home inspection, they had some cause for concern and had a mold test. They may have found an issue and had it corrected or had a test come back with good results, either way they closed on the house only to find a few weeks later visible mold on a wall in their basement.

Like the sewage line issue in the last chapter, this happens literally thousands of times each and every year in North America.

The possible outcomes are about the same as well. Perhaps the agent writes a check, but rarely. Almost never does the inspector, mold testing professional, or lab write a check to cover the issue. In most cases, the client is given the explanation and we leave it at that.

Then there's the solution, in this case and as this book is being written around 10% of the time, where your clients' problem is taken care of automatically. If they had a mold test with any company utilizing InspectorLab, they're covered. Look for one of these two logos in the marketplace:

MOLD|SAFE

MOLD|GARD

This is one of the other reasons I like companies that utilize InspectorLab, from a real estate transaction point of view. If your client moves in and did everything right, they should not have to pay for mold remediation if they find mold later. These policies cover the cleanup, so the results are guaranteed. (There is only one lab in the marketplace today that does this)

Let's take this a step further. The client benefit financially is obvious, but there is another important aspect here that will help you in explaining the mold issue to clients and reduce everyone's liability, and that would be simplification through a standard.

In guaranteeing the results, InspectorLab created a standard your client can go by. Without such a standard, they're right back to the internet and getting information overload from hundreds of sources. When one source delivers a guaranteed solution, the inclination to seek out all of these largely illegitimate sources of information drops substantially- offering clarity in the transaction and happier clients.

Chapter 4
Constant Marketing

Before we go into any more gaps, we need to focus on one thing: *None of this matters without clients*. What is your job as a real estate agent? To take care of your clients. Who should know how well you take care of your clients? *Everybody!*

You've probably heard every trick in the book about getting listings and selling buyers on using your services. You may have even heard of a marketing guru or two who will give you all the knowledge you need to know for only $499.00 a month!

Maybe that stuff works, I've certainly heard good reviews about some, but to me there's nothing better than being in the right place (everywhere) and at the right time (often) knowing what you're talking about and expressing it confidently.

I'm sure you have heard of the assumptive sale. It works in real estate as well. If you have a listing appointment or a meeting with a potential buyer, go in with the mindset that they are already your client and you are there to advise them on the next step. Armed with some of the lessons in this book about all the complexities of home inspection and home warranties, you're going to be able to tie in some things that your competition won't- and you'll be the instantly *credible expert*.

Getting your first client isn't the subject of this book. (We might touch on that in the next one) Keeping your existing clientele happy and getting referrals as a result is, and a big part of that involves keeping up with clients.

Friend them on Facebook, follow them on Twitter, Connect on LinkedIn...and make sure that when one of the gaps covered in this book or otherwise is solved by one of your solutions that you make a lot of noise about it. Your client will likely post or share their experience publicly as well if you let them know how they were uniquely protected. Their friends will ask themselves why they didn't have the same experience and you pick up a new client.

Another way to keep up with past clients: e-Newsletters.

A lot of people will tell you to do email campaigns, but not really give you content or a means by which to implement it. Others want to sell you their monthly subscription for marketing to your own clients.

I'm going to simplify all of that for you, sell you nothing, and make it real. My annual sales directly from emails are in the seven-figures, and I do not sell email marketing.

I give it away. So around 4500 of the top home inspection companies in North America.

Here's the best strategy for email marketing you as an agent. It's a two part strategy, one for potential clients and one for past clients. We will start with past clients because it is the easiest to implement.

Email marketing to past clients.

With the exception of a few investors you may work with, most clients won't purchase a home every month or even every year. You might hear from them every 5 to 7 years. The challenge there is that keeping up on the maintenance of an email marketing platform, paying the $19.99-$49.99 per month year after year, and either coming up with new content each month or purchasing that content for an additional fee month after month, can be taxing. (I realize some brokers offer a service like this, which is certainly convenient unless you switch offices at some point.)

Here's the bigger problem: After you pay all of this money and put all the time and effort into it, it still has a limited effect.

I've consulted with literally hundreds of real estate agents on email marketing and the results of their existing campaigns across the board were unanimously terrible. Open rates under 20%. Click rates under 1%. Opt-out rates over a 3 year period of 5% or more.

Content is the biggest challenge here.

Someone you just sold a home to last month doesn't want to hear about your new listings. Someone you sold a home to 7 years ago may now be in the market, but they've been ignoring your emails since you re-ran the cranberry salad recipe of '05.

Here's the biggest problem, as if it needed to get any worse- Let's say you put in the time and effort, paid the money, and you even put together some great content and had double the open rates of other agents in the market...we're still not talking about an incredible effect on your business. If you get a deal or two out of it per year, you're doing phenomenal. The ROI is terrible for most.

Now for the great news. Because the ROI is mediocre if you do everything perfectly and minimal if you don't, your competition in the marketplace have largely given up on the concept. At major email marketing companies, their servers are an endless graveyard of expired accounts evidencing the lack of enthusiasm many agents and other business owners have succumb to.

The fix is simple- use a premium inspection company offering RecallChek.

How this product works for you and your client is truly awesome and if you haven't taken advantage of its potential, you need to read this section closely.

Here's how it works. The inspector takes down the model numbers on appliances during the inspection and loads them into a system that automatically detects recalled items and finds free repairs on all of them- without exception (even if the manufacturer of the product isn't willing or able to make the repair). It's the only service of its kind and here's the best part for you: **Free email marketing for life.**

After your inspection, you will receive an email that instructs you to upload your photo and contact information. This will automatically be added to all of your past clients that have used any inspector with this logo:

Why is this better than traditional e-Newsletters? Two reasons-

1. **It's free and automatic, with content done for you, and it never stops.** You don't have to maintain anything- just keep your contact information up to date. That's it. (If you want to customize the content, view your client list and email events, you can, just contact your home inspector or click on the contact button in the application)

2. **The content is so relevant, it encourages more activity.** Who turns off an email with free repairs in it every month? Very few. This lifetime service never costs you or your client another penny, but around 1 in 10 of your clients will get a free repair or a brand new appliance as a result.

We started this chapter with a focus on promoting you as an agent, and in the process we found another gap- recalled items.

I've spoken all across the country to literally 15,000 or more real estate professionals and vendors, and on this recalled items issue the results are always the same when polling the room. I would ask, "How many in here would have a home inspection if they were buying a home or suggest a home inspection to clients buying a home?"

The answer is a unanimous yes, by show of hands typically.

I then ask, "How many of you would expect that your home inspector check the basic functions of kitchen appliances in the course of the home inspection?"

Again all hands go up.

My last question is a little more complicated: "If you were to have a home inspection, and the day after you moved in your house caught on fire because the oven malfunctioned, resulting from a known fire hazard that was public record, would that be something you thought your home inspector would find?"

Once again, a unanimous "yes" from the room. It seems logical to all of us in the industry, but it simply isn't the case across the board in home inspection.

In home inspection, you have a variety of licensing entities in some states and home inspection associations. Each has its own standards, and very few of them require that appliances be checked in the course of a home inspection. None of them requires appliances be checked for fire hazard and electrical hazard recalls.

The over 4500 inspection companies offering RecallChek do both, so they're a safe bet, but if you're working with someone else, ask if they're checking for both of these things for your clients. There are basically three types of inspectors in the market when it comes to appliances and recalls-some check appliances and deliver a RecallChek report (and that awesome email marketing platform) on every deal. Others may check appliances for function. Then at the very bottom of the inspection hierarchy there are inspectors who exclude appliances altogether from their process. These inspectors are failing to meet client expectations and often fall short in numerous other areas as well.

Where you see RecallChek, you can be confident your client will be taken care of. Watch out for inspectors who simply offer a link to your clients for consumer recalls- *they will never use it*, and it isn't accurate regardless.

In case you were wondering about that example of the oven catching on fire right after an inspection was done...it did happen. Just a few years ago in Roseville, California (outside Sacramento), and countless other times all around the country, always the result of choosing the wrong home inspector.

Client safety & satisfaction plus automatic email marketing appropriate for the audience (past clients) is definitely a no-brainer. Marketing to **potential** clients via e-Newsletters is a little more challenging.

Email marketing to potential clients.

"Sell. Sell. Sell."

We hear it all the time. Whether it is in the context of "always be marketing" or pushing metrics, the message has been the same for decades and probably centuries.

Over the last 10-15 years that message has changed dramatically, to the point of confusion. Now you hear things like "give first" and other phrases designed to get you to be passive in your marketing. The problem with this advice is that it is not qualified. (Not to say the source isn't qualified but rather that the advice itself lacked the specifics about the target necessary to make that determination.)

When we're talking about past clients, the absolute best way to handle them was described in the last section. It is passive, you're giving away free repairs and advice, you're keeping relevant content in front of your clients, you're keeping them safe, and you're selling nothing but results.

With "potential clients", it is okay and probably the best policy to go in for the kill. They signed in at an open house, joined your email list on your website, or met you face to face at a buyer's seminar. These are not people who joined your fan club to get the latest fashion trends and apple pie recipes in their email box. These are people who signed up with you because you sell real estate.

Give the people what they want.

Here's the content you should be delivering:

Listings. That simple.

Put together some of the hottest listings you have, blast them out to your list of potentials, and do so often. At least once a month if not once per week. At the beginning of each email, give the client a call to action about getting with you today because you have appointments available for their listing, they can get a free moving van when they buy and sell with you, or maybe that you're running a special where they can get a free home warranty when they close. Maybe you're having a client event and all are invited.

It's a simple concept and you can utilize existing templates in email services like Constant Contact, iContact, and MailChimp. Most agents will have less than 5,000 participants in these email lists at any given time, so you're looking at a minimal charge to run these campaigns.

When and if you ever switch providers, simply export your list.

Chapter 5
Damage Control

If it seems like the more business you do, the more you have to do to keep up, you're absolutely right and it isn't proportional. There's a science to it, as is often the case when 1 + 1 = 3.

The airlines have figured this out better than anyone. The next time you book a domestic flight, watch the patterns passengers create and how the airlines react. The first thing you will notice is that at check-in there are just less than enough people around during busy periods. Same thing with the kiosks. Then head to the gate...you're boarding at 4:00 PM for a 4:35 PM flight and no one is here at the desk at 3:15 PM. You wait 10 minutes, then 15, then finally around 3:45 PM you find the desk now has one or two people at it and you think you remember them from check-in.

None of this is by accident.

Thousands of times every single day (and probably 10's of thousands of times), a passenger enters the airport and sees a huge line of other passengers and thinks to himself/herself, "I guess it isn't worth it to get in that line to change/upgrade a seat". Countless others, even with the ability to check a bag for free, forego the process before they even witness it.

At the gate, where passengers wait with literally nothing to do but enjoy the least comfortable seating ever invented, the ability to go and chat up the gate crew is hindered by their palatable absence. Doesn't matter if the flight is on time, delayed, or even if they know there is about to be a huge plan-altering event for everyone there...no one is to be found.

Again the reasons are the same. With less availability comes less debate and minutia. If someone were parked at every gate all day long, 10's of thousands of additional requests involving changes, upgrades, rerouting, etc. would take place every single day, and due to the nature of the beast, most wouldn't be fulfilled. This would of course have a negative impact on the airline from a PR perspective, outweighing any potential positive they could experience from charging fees.

What the airlines have solved using scarcity, smaller businesses like mine and your real estate business solve with even more availability. Neither of us owns a monopoly on routes or participates in some oligopoly with few players or options. In my case, as a home warranty company, I am one of a dozen or more true national players who wants to earn your business, and as many as 30 in any individual market. In your case you're one of several hundred or even several thousand agents duly licensed and belonging to the local board. In your home inspector's case, there could be anywhere from 10 to 200 other options.

None of us has the luxury of locking all of our clients in a virtual jail cell behind a few government agents (TSA) where we can control the temperature, the availability of people, even the channel on the television, and worry about nothing more than not offending the customer so badly that they don't go to one of the other not much better options.

We (You and I) have to deliver a superior product each and every day, with more service, better transactions, and an overall better experience for the clients.

You do that in your business in ways that are very difficult to describe in any book this size. From open houses and dealing with closings, to finding the perfect home and getting to it quickly and negotiating a great deal. Your expertise is worth way more than any client pays you. Your generous giving of your time to your clients results in them demanding more and more of you as you grow.

Basically, if you build it, they will come (to complain about anything and everything and look for solutions to any and all of life's problems).

It happens in any personal service business. You're going to do everything at some point for your clients. Some may need a shoulder to cry on. Others need counseling. I saw an agent I knew well once in my neighborhood, and he was mowing a lawn. I stopped to ask him about it, and he had a simple explanation, "No, not starting a lawn mowing business. Had the time today and the client couldn't get it done before the open house. I figure all of the neighbors seeing me go the extra mile doesn't hurt either."

Great explanation, certainly not the norm for the industry, but I'm sure at some point you have gone way above and beyond for a client. All of this can be rather rewarding.

Dealing with complaints- not so much. Especially when the client feels you were the direct cause of the issue they are having.

Here's a scenario that happens literally every day in the market. Many times over. (We know it happens every day because we get this call on average more than once a day)

Another Gap in Real Estate: Home Inspection v. Home Warranty v. Contractor v. Seller

It's unique to North America, more specifically the U.S. and Canada, that home buyers have an expectation their repair costs in their "new" home (built long ago) will be zero dollars.

Some agents manage this expectation, but still the reality for the consumer is that everything in their world is insured. Homes, autos, even the televisions at Best Buy come with a warranty and you can extend it to 5 years at checkout.

Do clients expect a home warranty? Absolutely. In most areas, the uptake rate for warranties on owner occupied properties is over 90%. If you're not suggesting one, you're behind the rest of the market. Even in the markets where they're not insanely popular, they still are involved in a majority of transactions.

Do clients know what to expect from a home warranty? Not really. The average consumer doesn't know anything about home warranties or home inspections or real estate for that matter until they hear all about it from their real estate agent. You're in the business and you may not have known that whole thing about RecallChek and appliances from Chapter 4. Just imagine what the client really knows (or doesn't).

So here is their perception when any of the following occurs;

Buyer closes on home, moves in and within a couple months has an issue with any or all of the following-

- Air Conditioning

- Heating

- Plumbing

- An appliance

- The Electrical Panel

- A Water Heater

- Anything else mechanical.

The client does everything they were told. They call the 800 number on the back of their home warranty, and the home warranty company dispatches the contractor.

Contractor comes to home, charges the deductible or service call fee, and next thing you know he has taken apart an expensive system listed above. What happens next confuses the client.

"Well, your air conditioner is shot and needs to be replaced. This system doesn't match sizes on the inside or the outside, so they both need to be resized and since it wasn't a correctly installed system, the home warranty company says it isn't covered." – says the Contractor from the Home Warranty company.

The contractor goes on to say, "You just bought this house? Your home inspector should have told you this wasn't right…"

This example is real.

What I wrote above literally happens every day in this industry many, many times, and I could go into similar examples in all of the other mechanical components (i.e. sediment in a water heater tank or pitting on a bus bar in an electrical panel).

What I want to do right now is focus only on this air conditioning example. First, we'll start with the client perception.

What the client sees is a seemingly qualified HVAC technician, in a uniform, having been hired by a home warranty company, telling him something technical that seems to make sense (but he doesn't truly know for sure).

What the client feels is caught in the middle, because he sees everything as intertwined- his agent helped him find this house, the mortgage company helped finance it, at the title company it closed after being inspected by the home inspector, and now it is covered by the home warranty company listed on the settlement statement who then hired this contractor now standing in his kitchen giving him some bad news.

At this point, it doesn't matter whether you suggested one inspector or three to the client, everyone in the transaction just got tied back to you and the client has one question on his mind: **Who is**

responsible for this and what is my agent going to do about it?

Agents get this call all the time. It is like a bad joke around real estate offices. First a home inspector seems to nit-pick a house to death, now he missed something obvious...first a warranty company makes all sorts of promises and bought the office donuts and now they're not standing behind their policy, and so on. You can imagine the water cooler conversations about this one.

The ironic part- all of it was preventable and all of it was based on bad information.

Yes, this is something you should be sharing with all of your real estate agent friends right now. Wherever you are, if there is another real estate agent within shouting distance, stand up and yell at them to come over and read this with you, because if we could solve this gap in real estate the entire industry would be better off for it, and you will get more referrals when you have fewer disappointed clients.

Let's take apart what this contractor stated. Here's the quote again:

"Well, your air conditioner is shot and needs to be replaced. This system doesn't match sizes on the inside or the outside, so they both need to be resized and since it wasn't a correctly installed system, the home warranty company says it isn't covered." – says the Contractor from the Home Warranty company.

The contractor goes on to say, "You just bought this house? Your home inspector should have told you this wasn't right..."

Right off the bat, we're in trouble. "Air conditioner is shot" is not a diagnosis- it is a sales pitch. Regardless of the context, if you hear these words out of a mechanical contractor's mouth you should be firing them immediately. The air conditioning system, out of everything on the list, is one of the more complex and even this system is very simple.

You have a thermostat and control board that tells the unit to turn on and off. You have a condensing unit outside, with a compressor and coils, and inside you have an air handler and coil to transfer the cool temperature created by compressed refrigerant to the air.

"Shot" isn't a diagnosis. Either a motor has failed, a system has leaked, a component has failed, or the system is dirty. The diagnosis should be more specific than any of these categories, but the diagnosis should always fit into these categories.

Now we get to the mismatched components issue. For the contractor to suggest that "[the] home inspector should have [noted this]" is incorrect. Home inspectors don't generally go into capacity or sizing of units. Nonetheless, it operated on the day of the inspection and for the last ten years just fine and now suddenly it is a pre-existing condition and a cause for not covering a real mechanical malfunction that occurred today.

Of course we don't know what that mechanical malfunction is.

As an agent, this is the worst possible time for your phone to ring. The client is looking for answers and you're not an air conditioning expert (nor should you have to be).

This is pretty much the ultimate gap in real estate today. A solution here will be the difference between a client having an absolutely terrible homeownership experience and feeling tricked into a bad deal, or an outstanding experience where the client feels confident suggesting everyone in their sphere call you exclusively for all of their real estate needs.

This gap is so bad in fact that several agents I know have taken out their checkbooks and written the check on this one.

The solution here isn't to be like the airlines and ignore the phone call, offering up one of those cheesy voicemail messages that says you "return calls between 2 PM and 4 PM daily". It is a strategy, but it is a bad one.

The real solution is a combination of preventing the issue and outsourcing the administration of these complaints. Learning everything there is to know about heating and cooling, water heaters, electrical, and plumbing systems to begin with isn't something you should have to do as an agent. *Learning the standards of inspection and the various trades and how to apply all of this to a home warranty policy as well is something no one should have to do.*

Once again we find the biggest gaps coming from the home inspection and home warranty vendors, and once again the solution comes from the good ones- namely the Certified Inspection Experts throughout North America and Residential Warranty Services.

What if we could get a home inspector and a home warranty company to work together so that the client was never caught in the middle? It may seem like a simple concept, but it really didn't happen in the marketplace until the last few years.

You can completely eradicate the "your inspector (that your agent recommended) must have missed this so it isn't covered by the warranty company (that your agent recommended)" excuse and everything that comes along with it by simply doing two things;

1. Talk to your home inspector and home warranty company, and arrange a no preexisting conditions policy. If you're willing to give Residential Warranty Services a try for your clients, all you have to do is utilize one of the 4500+ Certified Inspection Experts in North America. Look for this logo:

2. Make sure your home inspector is offering the inspection warranty from RWS. Here's the logo to look for:

Here's where the transaction gets a lot easier for your client and where you can close a giant service gap and increase your referrals.

In the course of purchasing a home, there are basically four components involving the condition of the home;

- Seller's disclosure

- Home inspection

- Final walk-thru

- Home warranty

Each component has its advantages and disadvantages, but at the end of the day nothing ties them together in many transactions. The home inspector rarely sees the seller's disclosure, the home warranty company in most cases isn't familiar with the home inspector, and the walk-thru is generally just a cursory check by the buyer and agent.

When we can tie the home warranty to the home inspection in a meaningful way, and then add coverage to the inspection process that closes even more of the gaps that exist between the home inspection and the home warranty, the result is greater client satisfaction.

Here's another secret top real estate professionals utilize: longer than 12 month home warranties.

If you can deliver your client 14-18 months of coverage, that's something worth bragging about.

It is yet another way the client experience is better with you than it is with most agents in the market.

Chapter 6
Be Everywhere.
Pay Nothing.

In 5 short chapters we've covered all sorts of ground. Gaps between client expectations and inspection standards when it comes to appliances and recalls. Gaps between the home and the street in the form of expensive underground piping. Gaps in the HVAC, electrical, plumbing, and other mechanical systems in the home. Gaps in the transaction when it comes to ancillary services like mold testing.

All of these gaps, using the strategies in this book, are sealed completely and will now be an opportunity to market yourself rather than a referral-killing nightmare of a day. Client complaints now become opportunities.

Not one of these solutions costs you or your client anything. The 4500+ Certified Inspection Experts market themselves with competitive rates and Residential Warranty Services will even match prices from competitors.

When we set out to write this book, it was on the premise that I had conversations with agents all across North America- both one on one and in groups- where over 90% of the agents (and probably closer to 95%) heard everything said, asked questions, and the next day took the steps to make sure their clients didn't get stuck in one of these gaps.

Why would you ever utilize an inspector that doesn't guarantee his work with a warranty backed by a third party to ensure your client has a great experience?

Why would you ever consider using an inspector that doesn't check appliances at all when another in the market checks them thoroughly, finds any and all recalls, and ensures you are constantly in front of past clients forever with RecallChek?

Why would anyone ever risk their client lose thousands of dollars on a sewage line collapse when the top inspectors in the market all cover your clients with SewerGard?

Why would any agent ever risk their own liability and the fate of a transaction on mold testing advice from the internet when the leading companies offer the simplicity of InspectorLab reporting and guaranteed results?

Selfishly I would pose one more question...

Why would anyone choose a warranty other than Residential Warranty Services when their clients can experience an extended policy, no preexisting conditions, and underground sewer line coverage, when exactly 100% of the other options in the marketplace fail on all three accounts?

The answer is simple. We live in a relationship-based world. If we were in a vacuum, the pure rational and obvious nature of the statements above would make the choice easy for every buyer and agent in the market. Perhaps some aren't aware of the offerings available or don't have all the answers to questions they may have, but outside that small contingency those who don't use a particular product or service that is absolutely better than the other options in the marketplace fail to do so because they lack a connection to it.

This is why I put my personal email address right on the inside front cover of the book. Here it is again:

Nathan@Nathan.tv

There are over a million agents who might see the pages of this book, certainly several thousand will, and if every single one of them emailed me, I would cancel my plans for the weekend and respond to each and every one. That's how important making that connection is. Just as important, you need to be not just in one place- you need to be everywhere.

That's why the connection to your clients and potential clients with e-Newsletters, via social media, and in person is so important.

Let's add to that your online presence.

If a client or potential client were to search for you online right now, what would they find?

In many cases, in real estate, that connection has been hindered on the web. Most agents have one web site, and many of those web sites are part of an office site. Usually that site, like the agent search features at the board level, exclude contact information like email address, direct phone lines, and cell phone numbers.

The board doesn't want to give away your email address, which is totally understandable because agents are a target for all sorts of email sales gimmicks. Brokers may feel the same way.

Here's what you should do as a real estate agent:

Diversify.

Make it so anyone can find you, anywhere. Here's how you do it.

First, take advantage of any website options you have from your broker. Update your photo, add in all your qualifications, and put as much contact info in as is allowable.

Realize with your broker's website, if you work with one, is meant to get you business from visitors to the office website- not the other way around. (See below on how to create your own funnel websites to maximize your online presence)

Second, do the same for your online presence at the board level. Same goes for any other sites that list agents. You want to be the most accessible agent there!

Now to the slightly more difficult part. Build websites (plural) to capture every type of client you target market to. You should have one main site (for instance, www.Nathan.tv) and then other sites that target certain market segments. Perhaps one for condos, one for first time buyers, one for luxury residences. Depending on your market, there may be great opportunities in beachfront living or even large estates with horse stables. The sky is the limit.

What you don't want to do is spend thousands of dollars developing these sites, when most of the work involved is coming up with content anyhow. Just go to www.UltimateAgentWebsites.com and you're set. (You don't need to know how to build a website in order to use this) Five websites, including a builder and hosting, are free to real estate agents at that site.

There are certainly other options, most come with a fee, but take advantage of the free sites and any opportunity you have to get your name out there first.

Chapter 7
The Difference

When I started marketing home warranties over 15 years ago, I did so the old fashioned way. I had a policy written much like all the others in the market, I printed them by the thousands, and I went to real estate offices to "stuff boxes".

Relationships were all I had to go by, and luckily I had plenty of them. I hit a million in sales by my second year, which may as well have been a billion to a twenty year old. I felt like Donald Trump.

The following two or three years weren't nearly as good. Having tapped out all of the connections to real estate locally I already had, I found myself doing what every other company in the industry did: I marketed more. I hired a salesperson, did some direct mail, gave money to the local real estate board charities, attended every meeting I could.

Those next three years was a slow burn to get to $2-$3 million in sales. Still good, but nothing spectacular, and every day was hard work. I would put in 60-80 hours a week.

Then I discovered something that would change my home warranty business and the way we handled every aspect of the business forever- the USP.

USP stands for "Unique Selling Proposition". Think Domino's Pizza delivering your pizza in 30 minutes or less. The same concept can be applied to any business or service to make it uniquely better than other options, so we went about the daunting task of making our policies better than anything else out there.

We started partnering with brokers to offer E & O Deductible coverage. We added a "single deductible per malfunction" policy that to this day no other warranty offers. Then we added the only true no preexisting condition policy in the industry in cooperation with our network of Certified Inspection Experts. Our latest differentiator is the Sewer Line coverage, and once again the competition is far behind us.

Making this change accelerated our business and it can for you as well- in fact, you have an amazing opportunity as a real estate agent to be different than everyone else in your market.

What if every client was guaranteed a free home warranty? It would cost around $400 to be ahead of the competition.

How about a free moving truck? Perhaps a service guarantee where your commission is reduced if the home isn't sold in a certain period of time?

Any or all of these options make your advertisements and posts on social media more appealing, and nothing you do has to be permanent. Run a special first and see how it works.

Whatever you choose to offer, ask yourself this question:

"What makes your real estate business different than your competition?"

If the answer is something none (or very few) of your competitors would be willing to do, you're on to something!

Join the conversation at www.RealEstateMessageBoard.com.

Chapter 8
Resources

Throughout the book many things were mentioned, all resources you should at least be aware of as a real estate professional. This quick resource guide will summarize many of those items and give you links to find more information.

Home Warranty Resources

Home Warranty Coverage with no preexisting conditions, free extensions when using a qualified home inspector, and underground sewer line coverage for your clients.

RESIDENTIAL WARRANTY SERVICES, INC.

www.RWSwarranty.com

Coverage available in most all states, coming soon to every state in the U.S. and several locations in Canada.

In California, Home Warranties provided by:

RESIDENTIAL WARRANTY HOME PROTECTION OF CALIFORNIA

www.HomeWarrantyCalifornia.net

Home Inspection Resources

InspectionCentral.net – Find an inspector with a 100% satisfaction guarantee. All participants are Certified Inspection Experts offering a free extension to the Residential Warranty home warranty products.

PriorityMoldTest.com – Get a mold test or find a local mold testing company that offers guaranteed results from InspectorLab, along with a report that simplifies the process.

Things to look for in a home inspector to simplify your transaction and eliminate gaps:

1. RecallChek report provided on every transaction.

2. Inspection Warranty from Residential Warranty Services.

3. A genuine SewerGard policy.

4. Mold Testing through InspectorLab

5. Look for the Certified Inspection Expert logo

Web Resource for Agents

UltimateAgentWebsites.com – free website builder and hosting for real estate agents. Five free websites.

RealEstateMessageBoard.com – Get immediate feedback on questions, discuss issues with other real estate professionals, and increase your SEO by adding your URL to your signature line.

More Information & Supplies

Get any of the following:

- Book a sales presentations

- Get brochures and fliers for your office

- More copies of this book

- Questions answered regarding any products and services

Simply by emailing Nathan@Nathan.tv

Thanks for being a Savvy Agent!

RESIDENTIAL WARRANTY SERVICES, INC.
HOME WARRANTY
simple.
as it should be.
NO
PRE-EXISTING
CONDITIONS
WHEN YOU USE A
CERTIFIED INSPECTION
EXPERT
CERTIFIED
INSPECTION
EXPERT
ORDER YOUR HOME WARRANTY TODAY
AT 800-544-8156 OR VISIT RWSWARRANTY.COM

Websites exclusively for Real Estate Agents

Build up to five free sites!

UltimateAgentWebsites.com

The Savvy Agent:
Increase your Referrals and Eliminate Liability
1st Edition
By P. Nathan Thornberry

Residential Warranty Services
The Inspector Services Group
2015

*Any and all marks are the property of their
respective companies.*